Jesus as a Boy

By Cristina Marques

SCANDINAVIA

INTRODUCTION

Jesus said, "Become like little children." The Children of the Bible series puts attention on the littlest of Jesus' flock. Each of these characters has an inspiring story to tell. God used their lives to teach the world about his love. As you read these stories aloud, remember God's presence inside every child's spirit. The simplest stories sometimes hold the greatest power. May these stories be the beginning of a lifelong love of the Bible for your children. There is treasure to gain for young and old alike.

To: Ellie
From: Uncle Richard
        and
    Aunt Carol
        and
    Your friend,
    James, Jr. (JR)

Just like you and me, Jesus was a child, too! But he was no ordinary child. There was something special about Jesus.

Jesus was born on a starry night in Bethlehem. He was born in a stable near the animals. His parents, Mary and Joseph, were happy to welcome him. Even the angels worshiped him. They knew that Jesus was the Son of God.

Jesus was a busy boy.
He loved to help Joseph
with his carpentry.
He loved to help his
mother, too. But most
of all, Jesus loved to
learn about God. He
grew wiser everyday.

When Jesus was 12 years old, he went on a trip with his parents. They were going to Jerusalem for Passover. Passover was a special festival to give God thanks. Jesus could hardly wait.

When the festival was over, Mary and Joseph headed home with a crowd of people. Suddenly they looked around for Jesus. Where was he?

Not a single person they asked had seen Jesus. They ran back and forth on the road looking for him. Finally they turned back towards Jerusalem. Jesus' parents were very worried.

After three days, they finally found Jesus. He was in the temple learning and teaching others about God. Even the elders were asking him questions. Everyone was amazed by his wisdom.

Mary and Joseph hugged Jesus. Then Jesus asked them, "Didn't you know I would be in my Father's house?" Mary was proud of her boy. She thanked God that Jesus understood who he was.

Jesus learned more about his Father God everyday. Knowing God made him wise.

JESUS AS A BOY – WISDOM

Jesus was God's son. God's temple was Jesus' home, too.
He loved to go there and learn. But Jesus did not just
want to be smart. He didn't just want to know things.
He wanted to know God. Jesus knew the only way to
understand God was through wisdom. Wisdom is knowing
things with the heart. When we read the Bible, pray,
or worship in church, we will know God, too. God gives
wisdom to those who seek him.

© Scandinavia Publishing House
Drejervej 15,3 DK - Copenhagen NV Denmark
Tel. (+45) 3531 0330
www.scanpublishing.dk
info@scanpublishing.dk
All rights reserved.

Text: Cristina Marques
Illustrations and graphic design:
Belli Studio, Gao Hanyu
Translation: Ruth Marschalek, Lissa Jensen

Printed in China
ISBN: 978 87 7247 179 2